# A Round-Table in Poictesme

## A Symposium

Edited by
DON BREGENZER
and
SAMUEL LOVEMAN

*What is a book?   A series of little
printed signs,—essentially only that.
It is for the reader to supply himself
the forms and colors and sentiments
to which these signs correspond.   It
will depend on him whether the book
be dull or brilliant, hot with passion
or cold as ice.*
—ANATOLE FRANCE

WILDSIDE PRESS

www.wildsidepress.com

Published by
Wildside Press, LLC
P.O. Box 301
Holicong, PA 18928-0301 USA
www.wildsidepress.com

Wildside Press Edition: MMIII

# Contents

# Contents [CONTINUED]

# A Foreword

IN JUSTICE to the reader of this symposium the Editors desire to state that the occasion for the publication of these papers arises from a feeling on the part of members of The Colophon Club that comparatively little has been done in appreciation of the life-long sacrifice and assiduity of James Branch Cabell to creative literature.

Instances of the neglect of literary artists are not uncommon—especially in America. Herman Melville, saddened by the attitude of his contemporaries that almost openly proclaimed him a pariah, drew his mantle about him in his later years, and died embittered—convinced that posterity held little for him beyond the mere linking of his name with that of the transcendental Hawthorne. To Ambrose Bierce, now an acknowledged master of the short story, recognition came slowly. In the non-acceptance of Edgar Saltus lies the epitomized tragedy of an entirely unrecognized man of genius.

With Mr. Cabell we have come perilously

close to a repetition of the old story. It is in an effort to forestall any recurrence of such a public misfortune that this collection of papers, with Mr. Cabell's own unselfish contribution, is offered as a permanent tribute.

Thanks and obligations are due to the friends and contributors that have made possible such a measure of appreciation. Gratitude is expressed for the voluntary assistance given by Mr. H. L. Mencken, Mr. Christopher Morley, Mr. Ben Ray Redman, Mr. Ernest Boyd and Mr. Burton Rascoe as evidenced by their various contributions; thanks, again, to Robert M. McBride & Company in general, and Mr. Guy Holt in particular, for permission to reprint certain excerpts from Mr. Cabell's published work, and to the editors of *The Reviewer* for the use of Mr. Redman's essay, *Bülg the Forgotten*, first published in that magazine.

Enduring gratitude is tendered to Mr. Cabell, without whose friendly support and generous co-operation this publication would not have been possible. Mr. Cabell, be it

A Foreword

said, requested that his contribution appear
as the last item in these pages, upon the
ground of some natural unwillingness to seem
to lead and marshal a procession which brought
tribute to him. We have, none the less, esteem-
ed it preferable to place this peculiarly revela-
tory paper first.

—THE EDITORS

Cleveland,
January 13, 1924.

"I see", said the Queen, "or rather in this darkness, I cannot see at all, but I perceive your point. Your opening interests me—and you may go on."

—*Jurgen.*

# A Round-Table in
# Poictesme

# The Author of
# The Eagle's Shadow

BY

JAMES BRANCH CABELL

Some men there must be in every age and every land of whom life claims nothing very insistently save that they write perfectly of beautiful happenings.
—*The Certain Hour.*

# The Author of
# The Eagle's Shadow

**M**OST writers, for their sins, are used to the incursions of the literarily-inclined young man (with, as a rule, quite dreadful manuscripts hidden about his person) who wants advice as to his life work. But that this especial young man should be calling upon me for that purpose, or for any other purpose, did, I confess, astonish me . . . .

For he dropped in the other evening. He was fat, remarkably fat for a lad of twenty-two or thereabouts; and he had, as I noticed first of all, most enviably thick hair, sleeked down and parted "on the side", with some fanfaronade in the way of capillary flourishes. He was rather curiously dressed, too, I considered: the lapels of his coat were so small and stiff; they were held in place, I deduced, by a coat-spring: and he wore a fawn-colored waistcoat, and his rigorous collar towered, incredible in height, above a sky-blue "Ascot tie", which was resplendently secured with a largish sword-hilt asparkle everywhere with diamonds. It must have been, in fine, a good twenty years since I had seen anybody appareled quite as he was  . . . .

"I have just sold three stories to magazines," he announced, "and I was wondering, sir, if you would advise me to become a regular writer now."

To that I gave my customary, sage and carefully considered reply.    "Of course," I informed him, "there is a great deal to be said upon both sides."

"I wrote five, you see; and I mailed them all out together. And *The Smart Set* took one; and *The Argosy* took the one I sent them, too; and Mr. Alden wrote me a real nice letter about the one I sent *Harper's*, and said they would be very glad to use it if I would let them say 'paunch' where I had written 'belly'. That's all right, of course, though you do sort of think of Falstaff as having one. But the other two came back, although I can't see why, when you look at the stuff those very magazines—!"

"You will see, by and by," I assured him; "and then you will wonder about the stories that did not come back."

"Anyhow, I got a hundred and five dollars for the lot of them. Yes, sir, not a cent less. And to have three out of five stick, the very first time, is pretty unusual, don't you think?"

To that I assented. "It is the bait in the trap, it is the stroke of doom, it is the tasted pomegranate of Persephone."

"Then I have the notion for a book, too. It's about a young man who is in love with a girl—"

"That now is a good idea. It is an idea that has possibilities."

"—Only, he can't ask her to marry him, because she has lots of money, and he is poor. Of course, though, it all comes out all right in the end. His uncle left another will, you see."

"Now was that will, by any chance," I wondered, "discovered long years afterward in the secret drawer of an old desk? And did it transform your high-minded but impoverished hero into a multi-millionaire?"

And the young man asked, "Why, how did you know?"

"It is not always possible to explain these divinations. Such flashes of imaginative clairvoyance just incommunicably come to me sometimes."

He considered this. He said, with a droll sort of awe, "Probably you do think of things quicker after you have been writing so long—"

I shook my head morosely. "Quite the contrary."

"And of course you have written so many books that— You see, I naturally read them, on account of our similarity in names—"

"You liked them, I hope?"

Very rarely have I seen any young man counterfeit enthusiasm less convincingly. "Why, how can you ask that, I wonder! when everybody knows that your books, sir—!"

"Come, come!" I heartened him, "I have been reviewed a great deal, remember! The production of articles as to my plagiarisms and obscenities ranks as a national industry. Very lately Judge Leonard Doughty exposed me to all Texas as a chancre-laden rat whose ancestry had mixed and simmered in the devil's cauldron of Middle Europe. And, besides, since Professor Fred L. Pattee let the news get out, in perfectly public print, that I am dead and my soul is already in hell, there does not seem much left for any moderately optimistic person to be afraid of."

"Well, but," the young man pointed out, "I'm not unbiased. There is so much about me in your books, you see, sir; and you do make me seem sort of funny. You sort of keep poking fun at me."

"I know. But I cannot help it. For you appear to me, I confess, the most ridiculous person save one that I have ever known. I am the other person."

"Well, I am afraid I don't entirely like your books, sir," he conceded.

And I sat looking at him, both amused and saddened. For never until tonight had it occurred to me how utterly would this especial young man dislike my books if ever he could know of them. And he was trying so hard, too, to be polite about it.

"Why do you do it, sir," the boy asked now, almost reproachfully. "You get a plenty of pleasure out of life, don't you? and what did you want, anyhow, that you never got?"

"Yes: and I don't know," I admitted, seriatim.

"Well, then, why don't you write some books that will make people see the world is a pretty good sort of place after all?"

"But surely it does not require two persons to point out such an obvious geographical feature? Cannot posterity rely upon you, by and by, to diffuse that truism single-handed?"

"I certainly do hope so," he replied. Now his voice changed. "For I would like to write the very nicest sort of books—like Henry Harland's and Justus Miles Forman's and Anthony Hope's. They would be about beautiful, fine girls and really splendid young men, and everything would come out all right in the end, so they could get married, and not be sort of bitter and smart-alecky and depress people the way"—he coughed,— "the way some people do."

"Young man," I started out, severely, "it is quite evident you are not married—"

To which he countered, now I think of it, rather staggeringly. "But you, sir, are not in love. You never will be, sir, not ever any more."

I said: "Yes; that does make a difference. I remember." Then I said: "Stop talking bosh! and stop calling me 'sir'! I'm not your grandfather. It is rather the other way round. And, besides, we were talking about books. Well, you may try, if you like, to write the blithering kind of novel you describe. But, somehow, I don't think you will ever succeed at it."

"You ought to know best, sir, of course, about my abilities. And so, if you would honestly advise me— Still, I would certainly like to be a real author—"

He was looking at me now, across that quite remarkable blue tie and shiny sword-hilt, with very touching deference, and with, of all conceivable emotions, envy. I understood, with the most quaint of shocks, that I possessed every one of the things which this preposterous young fellow wanted. I had written and published, sometimes even with commercial extenuation, at least as many magazine stories and books as he hoped by and by to have to his credit: I could imagine how my comfortable-looking large home, and my ownership of actual stocks and bonds, and my acquaintance with a number of more or less distinguished persons, would figure in his callow mild eyes: and I had tasted, too, if not of fame, most certainly of all the notoriety he ever aspired to. Why, but what does it not seem to this pathetic boy, I reflected, actually to have one's picture in the papers! For I would well remember certain ancient glancings toward that awesome pinnacle of being a celebrity.

I was, in fine, by this boy's standards, a success. I had today each one of the things he had ever consciously desired. That really was a rather terrible reflection.   .   .   .

But he was speaking. "Then you would honestly advise me, sir, not to take up writing as a regular thing?"

"I don't see how I can advise you that— not honestly, at least. For you will get out of the writing all—heaven help you!—that you hope to get."

"Why, then—" He was abeam.

"You simply wait until you have got it! You can attend to your grinning then, if you feel like it. For you will get every one of the things you think you want. Only, you will get them by the, upon the whole, most philanthropic process of not ever writing any of the mush which you now plan to write."

"But I don't understand—"

"Nor do I, either, quite. But from the start will be tugging at your pen a pig-headed imp that will be guiding it his way instead of the way you intended. And with each book he will be growing stronger and more importunate and more cunning, and he will be stealing the pen away from you for longer and longer intervals. And by and by that imp, full grown now and the very devil of a taskmaster, will be dictating your books from beginning to end—not to speak here of his making you sweat blood when you revise, at his orders, all the earlier ones."

"Come, now,"—and the young fellow was looking at me rather like a troubled cow,— "come, now, sir, but you don't really mean I am going to be possessed by a devil?"

"Some people will put it that way, only a bit less politely. But I would say, by a daemon. Socrates had one, you may remember."

"Yes, but this one—?"

"You," I replied, "will call him the desire to write perfectly of beautiful happenings. Other persons will call him quite different things. Anyhow, with time, you will fall into a sort of bedrugging daemon-worship, and you will go the way he commands you, without resisting any longer. It will be most deplorable. So Professor Henry A. Beers will have, after all, to dismiss your literary claims from the pale of serious consideration, because you are not of Colonial stock—"

"But, sir, my father's people came in 1727, and my mother's in 1619—!"

"That will not matter. Facts are but reeds in the wind of moral indignation. And Maurice Hewlett must become very cuttingly sarcastic about your being a Jew brought up on the Talmud—"

"Me, sir?"

"Most certainly, you. And a transfigured Richard le Gallienne, purified by his intellectual death and descent into the helotage of reviewing, will be compelled to unmask you as a moral and spiritual hooligan with a diminutive and unkempt and unsavory ego. Altogether, you perceive, you will get, through this daemon-worship, into some trouble."

Very rarely have I seen any young man more unaffectedly appalled. "But look here, sir! I don't want to get into any trouble. I simply want to contribute to the best magazines, and write some wholesome and nice entertaining books, that will sell like *The Cardinal's Snuff-Box* and *The Prisoner of Zenda.*"

"I know. It is rather funny that you should begin with just those goals in view. You will not ever attain them. That will not matter so much—after a while. But what will very vitally matter—to you, anyhow,—is that, having once meddled with the desire to write perfectly of beautiful happenings, you will not ever be able to forswear your daemon. And such folly is, of course, enough to set every really well-thought-of person in America braying. So that in time—who knows?— you too may come to be a chancre-laden rat, and a German Jew with a soul in hell and simmered ancestors and a notoriously unkempt ego, and may otherwise help out with the week's literary gossip."

Whereon the young man rose; and he remarked, with a perhaps not wholly unwarranted uncertainty, "Then you advise me, sir—?"

"I cannot advise you the one way or the other. I am merely forewarning you that, if you insist upon writing books, you will get what you wanted."

He smiled now, brightly, intimately, strangely. "I see: but isn't that also in the one way which matters," he demanded of me, "true?"

And I smiled back at him. "Yes," I admitted, "it seems true in the one way which matters, also."

"Why, then," said he, "I reckon I had better keep right on with *The Eagle's Shadow*".

And after that he went quite suddenly away. He returned, I imagine, to 1902 or thereabouts.

I hope he did, for his sake. There was a rather nice girl awaiting him, back there in

1902.    Then, in addition to her, he would have the facile, false inspirations of *The Eagle's Shadow* to play with, I reflected, as I resumed my sober pruning of over-frequent "that's" from the last proof-sheets of *The High Place.*

# *Cabell versus Cabell and Others*

BY

ERNEST BOYD

"Intelligent persons do not attempt to keep abreast of modern fiction.  It is probably ascribable to the fact that they enjoy being intelligent, and wish to remain so".
—*The Cords of Vanity*

# *Cabell versus Cabell and Others*

THE novels and stories of James Branch Cabell are usually classified in three groups, historical, mythical and contemporary, and apparently almost everyone is agreed that the least important of these are the contemporary. The plaintiffs in the case are *The Eagle's Shadow*, *The Cords of Vanity*, *The Rivet in Grandfather's Neck* and *The Cream of the Jest*, and against them are arrayed the author himself, the imposing list of his other admirable works, and the testimony of a host of his admirers. I do not say that these books have not been mentioned with appreciation by some of his critics, particularly *The Cream of the Jest*, but they have also been dismissed with a singular lack of discernment by those whose enthusiasm for Cabell cannot be doubted. In general there is a disposition to relegate these studies of contemporary manners to a position far subordinate to that of his other work.

Although Cabell seems to agree with this

evaluation, and has adopted an almost apologetic—certainly a condescending—tone towards the two earliest on their re-issue, I believe that this attitude, in the majority of cases, can be explained by extraneous circumstances, to-wit, by the suppression of *Jurgen*. It was that book which, for a variety of reasons not altogether literary, made James Branch Cabell famous, and those who then discovered him naturally looked in his previous and subsequent writings for those elements which pleased them in *Jurgen*. It has always seemed to me that an author can best and most fairly be judged only when his work is considered chronologically, that is to say, in the order of his own growth and development.   Then it becomes possible to single out one's preferences and to justify them by reference to his general evolution. So far as Cabell is concerned that was rendered difficult by the great notoriety of one book, which threw his entire achievement out of perspective, and by the fact that two of the books in the group which I am considering were almost unprocurable.

It is a significant fact, in this connection,

that *The Eagle's Shadow* was enthusiastically reviewed by Percival Pollard, a critic who was admittedly unorthodox and ahead of his time, whereas Hugh Walpole in *The Art of James Branch Cabell* declares that it is an early work which "need not detain us", the classical phrase on such occasions, when politeness suggests that discretion is the better part of criticism.    Walpole is unaware that this book was published in England at the time of its first appearance, as was also *The Cords of Vanity*, for in the same pamphlet he says: "*The Certain Hour* is, I believe, the only book by Mr. Cabell yet published in England". The truth is, of course, that almost all of Cabell's works were issued in New York and London simultaneously, but there as here they did not attract the attention which was centered upon them once *Jurgen* was suppressed.    That *The Eagle's Shadow* detained American readers, to the extent of arousing a vastly comic indignation, is evident from the appendix to the recent revised edition, where the flutterings of the moralists of the 1904 vintage are recorded.    When Heinemann published it in London it did not arouse even that kind of comment.

Hugh Walpole is perhaps the most prominent spokesman whom I can quote in support of the theory that the contemporary novel is not Cabell's field, and for that reason it is necessary to establish the fact that his discovery belongs to the order I have described. The works of James Branch Cabell have been available in England from the beginning, but he was not even a name to his English critic and admirer, who did not know that his novels could be obtained in the London circulating libraries. Consequently, granted my theory, I was not surprised to find Walpole saying that "the modern novels", namely *The Eagle's Shadow*, *The Cords of Vanity* and *The Rivet in Grandfather's Neck*, are "of all the books" "most vulnerable to attack". "They must seem", he writes, "to the reader who picks them up casually, confused, unpleasant and uncompleted". The heroine of *The Rivet* is "irrational and spasmodic". Whereupon he proceeds to sum up the case against the plaintiff in the present appeal:

"All this is simply to emphasize that Cabell is not a modern realist. In *Beyond Life* which is his magnificent, unequivocal, defiant testament, he proclaims again and again that he is not. We have had quite enough in modern criticism of the determination of critics to force writers into some shape or form that they could never possibly support. There is no need to commit this crime over Cabell, but it is a legitimate criticism, I think, that, being what he is, he would be wiser to leave alone themes that demand realism and psychological analysis for true revelation."

What is most interesting in this comment is the curious assumption that, when Cabell turns from cloak and sword romances and mythical sagas then he must become a "modern realist". Obviously this is an artificial dilemma, and it is only when one allows Cabell—or when he allows himself!—to be maneuvered between the horns of that dilemma that such works as *The Rivet in Grandfather's Neck* and *The Cords of Vanity* (not to mention *The Cream of the Jest,* which Hugh Walpole does not classify as modern) can be set aside as inadequate or unworthy of the same attention as *Domnei* or *The High Place*. So far as I am aware nobody has ever maintained that Anatole France is a modern realist, but the four volumes of *L' Histoire contemporaine* are assuredly neither in the historical nor the mythical categories into which his work, by analogy with that of Cabell, may be divided. When I first read *The Rivet* my feeling was that a satire on the South had been written in the manner of France's satire on the Third French Republic. Not only in that manner, but with so much of the great Frenchman's superb irony and subtle humor, that it did not require *Jurgen* to convince me that James Branch Cabell was a literary craftsman of the first order. The very defects of Cabell's modern novels, when judged by the test of realism, are those of Anatole France; the "irrational and spasmodic" heroines, the tendency "to cover up weak spots with a motto, an epigram, a footnote"—to quote Hugh Walpole again. In brief, the peculiar virtues and weaknesses of a novelist who is a satirist of the comedy of manners rather than an analyst concerned with the depths of the soul. It is, of course, possible to argue that *The Elm Tree on the Mall, The Wicker-Work Woman, The Amethyst Ring* and *M. Bergeret in Paris* are not novels. They are not, in the sense that *Father Goriot* and *L'Assommoir* are novels, but they are certainly not amongst the lesser works of Anatole France, on that account, for they are amongst the immortal prose of modern French literature.

In speaking of *The Cream of the Jest* Burton Rascoe has rightly mentioned Anatole France as a comparison, and it is on the affinity between the Cabell of the four volumes of contemporary American manners and the author of the four volumes of French Contemporary History that I wish to insist. Whether they are realists, whatever be their psychological blindness, they are both deft ironists who play with the spectacle of the life about them in a style which is an enchantment. Both have shown themselves masters in works as disparate as *The Eagle's Shadow* and *Jurgen,* as *The Crime of Sylvestre Bonnard* and *At the Sign of the Reine Pedauque,* and the reproaches of immorality, of superficiality, of lack of sentiment, of rudimentary psychology, have been brought against each of them by various types of criticism. Their attitude towards women has been severely reproved by all romanticists. The creator of Sylvestre Bonnard and M. Bergeret, of Jerome Coignard and Thais, can interest me in all these "figures of earth", and I have an equal sympathy for Robert Etheridge Townsend, Felix Bulmer Kennaston and Jurgen the pawnbroker, for Manuel the Redeemer and Margaret Hugonin, that adorable blonde. Am I too catholic? Do I champion a lost cause? Well, I submit that when a first novel has so elusive and excellent a title as *The Eagle's Shadow*, and when the author can follow it up with another so skilfully named as *The Rivet in Grandfather's Neck*, and when he caps these with *The Cream of the Jest*—then, realism or no realism, I feel that he is not altogether unequipped to write just that sort of modern novel which James Branch Cabell alone has achieved in America.

*A Practitioner in Perfection*

BY

DON BREGENZER

Off-hand I would say that books are best insured against oblivion through practise of the auctorial virtues of distinction and clarity, of beauty and symmetry, of tenderness and truth and urbanity.

—*Beyond Life.*

# A
## Practitioner in Perfection

OMEONE has well said that the case of James Branch Cabell belongs to comedy in the grand manner. For fifteen years the man wrote—and wrote superbly well—unrecognized save by the few members of a cult of appreciative admirers. To illustrate the dearth of discerning readers and to give an illuminating idea of the average critical intelligence of American book-reviewers, let us glance for a moment at some of the opinions of the Fourth Estate regarding Cabell. For these we would refer you to the pages immediately following the conclusion of *Beyond Life* (second edition), which contain some "critical" (God help us!) reviews of Cabell's books. These range from a dictum like, "told in a blundering, disorderly fashion", said of that delightful volume, *The Cream of the Jest*, by a brilliant reviewer of *The New York Tribune*, to that omniscience evidenced by the blithe statement, "Mr. Cabell is not a literary artist", sponsored by *The Philadelphia Press* in speaking of *The Line of Love,* a collection of some of the finest short stories of our time.

Really, such inane judgments would not be so regrettable had these and the even more fatuous comments of other critics, every bit as sapient, not been believed by an army of credulous readers. As a result, one by one as written and issued, the works of the most distinguished American author of the present time gathered dust on the book-shop shelves. And as quite apropos of the general reading public, we might here include a paraphrase of Dr. Johnson's well-known verse on Tea addressed to Mrs. Thrale:

> "But hear, alas! this mournful truth,
> Nor hear it with a frown,—
> Thou canst not write the bunk so fast
> As we can gulp it down!"

Secure in the knowledge that his work promised to be endowed with permanence, however, Cabell quite realized that the Victorian ideals of America were responsible for this lamentable condition. He therefore elected to ignore the idiotic reviewers. And by the way, if these critics (so-called by courtesy) feel that Cabell's contempt for them amounts to the barbarous, perhaps there is a greater share of barbarism than they suspect in their scorn of him! Yet even the most stupid critic that continually cavils at Cabell must, if he reads the man's works with as unbiased a mind as he can summon, gradually acquire the notion that there is a deal more clever irony, devastating wit, historical lore, sound erudition, superb imagination, excellent poetry and impeccable writing in them than he had ever suspected.

Thinking that they had permanently cast Cabell into Coventry, and that henceforth his pen would be as one writing in the wilderness, these censorious vaqueros continued their canterings in critical fields. Then in 1919 Cabell's publishers issued his twelfth book—a volume called *Jurgen*. Three months after its appearance it was suppressed upon the say-so of one John S. Sumner (the Peeping Tom of Literature), because he claimed that it contained obscenities (God save the mark!). The suppression, and its subsequent publicity, for the nonce catapulted Cabell into something resembling popularity. In passing, I might mention that upon the release of the book from Limbo, four years after its incarceration, it sold some 30,000 copies; and we wager that at least 28,650 of that number neatly shot that many readers through the upper nap of the crowns of their respective chapeaux. So much for the Sumnerian jahad!

Well, Cabell, as we say, reached something approximating popularity. His work even as early as 1904 had been issued across the water under a London imprint. It was not until later (circa 1919), however, that several discerning English critics went so far as to say something to the effect that "the fellow writes rather decently well". Now it is a well-known fact that every time the English critics take snuff, the American critics sneeze. So, as usual obeying this trans-Atlantic gesture with alacrity, these critical dons and book surveyors recanted their former opinions as to Cabell being a mediocre scribbler, and hastened pell-mell into the English band-wagon. Then singing Cabell's praises more loudly than they had ever sung those of any other current American author (in order, no doubt, to make amends for their sins of commission in the past) these professors and reviewers tardily did their share to elevate him to his present high niche in American letters.

Now just what sort of writer is this Cabell, whom the title of this paper describes as "Practitioner in Perfection?" Well, in the introduction to his translation of *The Crime of Sylvestre Bonnard*, Lafcadio Hearn says: "—if by Romanticism we understand that unconscious tendency of the artist to elevate truth itself beyond the range of the familiar, and into the emotional realm of aspiration, then Anatole France is betimes a romantic". Hearn wrote these words in 1890, when the great Frenchman was at the flood-tide of his genius. Change the name of Anatole France in this quotation to that of James Branch Cabell, and it may stand as truthfully correct as before. Cabell *is* an incurable Romanticist—and hence an implacable foe of Realism. He is a deal more interested in the aspirations of the owners of flaming sceptres, flashing sword-blades, hose and doublets, patches, fans and powdered hair, than in the dirt in the boudoirs of the lowly or the sex repressions of factory hands—

subjects of the sort most dear to the heart of your Realist!

And what, it may be asked, urges Cabell to write? Briefly, it is that "obscure, inner necessity", mentioned by Conrad—and conceivably, of course, Cabell wishes only as a reward that in each of his completed productions he may, with unbiased judgment, have a quite justifiable personal pride and joy. For Cabell is the example, par excellence, of the artist with an artist's conscience. He is ever attempting to improve his books. He writes—then re-writes—and re-writes once more. Like Flaubert, he searches always for *le mot juste*.

Lest we be accused of exaggerating this particular point, we recommend that you read *The Line of Love* in the original edition of 1905, and at the same time compare it with the revised edition issued in 1921. The changes are slight and meticulous rather than structural or sweeping—a phrase added here, a sentence deleted there; a word transposed here, a melodious adjective substituted for one that seems dissonant. And all this done in order that the rhythm may attain nearer perfection. For Cabell has learned much in the twenty years since the birth of his first book. His work gives evidence of a quiet but steady progress toward the goal of the true literary artist, which is, as he well says in his own words, "always to write perfectly of beautiful happenings". And that reader must indeed be troubled with myopia, who does not have evoked for him on every page, evidence of Cabell's attainment of this admirable and cherished ideal.

Let petty critics caterwaul that his style shows preciosity—that his work lacks content —that his writings have not a plenitude of ideas. At the most these cavilers refer to peccadilloes. Cabell's style is too natural to be considered precieux, for it is charming and substantial language gracefully woven into a beautiful, multi-colored word tapestry by a supreme word-artist—in brief, a spontaneous style. As to lack of content, content with Cabell is always secondary, for he quite realizes that style is all-important if a work is to be immortal. And as to dearth of ideas, few writers of Romance have possessed such a completely filled Fortunatus's

purse of ideas—ideas that are always sound,
frequently delightful, invariably interesting—
and thank God—never banal.

To the reader who is discerning enough to
have read the entire canon of Cabell's work
there is clearly unfolded the great, imaginative
scheme underlying his writings.     Like
Balzac and his *Comedie Humaine*, Cabell has
produced his own lineage of fictional characters—a lineage that finds its earliest recorded beginnings in the year 1234, when
Dom Manuel (from whom all Cabellian
characters claim common descent) met Mira-
mon Lluagor at the pool of Haranton, and
comes down without a break to the present
century to the incidents described in *The Eagle's
Shadow* and *The Rivet in Grandfather's Neck*. As
Cabell himself says, "My books constitute
a largish family tree"—and he might in fair
justice add, "and a magnificent romantic
epic."

Bonaparte, it is said, had a room where he
was used to recline on a sofa and gaze upon
a window painted with the escutcheons of his
vassal monarchs.    Evidently Cabell, before
commencing his writing career, gazed upon

the windows of his imagination whereon were painted the figures, real and imaginary, that some day were destined to move so vividly through his colorful pages. And taken all in all, they comprise a glittering, unforgetable, kaleidoscopic pageant consisting of Kings, Queens, Princes, Princesses, Counts, Duchesses, Lords, Earls, Marquises and other protagonists, upon whom it has pleased Cabell to confer noble titles conjured up from his own fancy. Then by the clever manipulation of the images of mud modelled by Manuel in *Figures of Earth*, Cabell, with sound artistry, smoothly interpolates into this genealogical pageant the well-known historico-literary figures of Alessandro de Medici, Shakespeare, Herrick, Pope, Wycherley, and Richard Brinsley Sheridan. These personages are depicted to the life in that volume of superb short stories, *The Certain Hour*.

Let no one imagine that the many charming and interesting consanguineous people in this kinetic panorama are mere marionettes, moved about by strings in the hands of their creator, as in a Punchinello show. *Per contra*, all are flesh and blood characters that need no artificial breath blown into them by an author's bellows, for they think, talk and act as human beings. They are impinged vividly upon the reader's imagination as people the reader would like to meet and converse with regarding the problems of social and moral conduct through which Cabell artistically and successfully pilots them. To mention only a few of these people, there are Cynthia Allonby and Matthiette in *The Line of Love*; King Edward I of England and Queen Philippa in *Chivalry*; Perion and Melicent in *The Soul of Melicent* (now known as *Domnei*); Lady Drogheda and Wycherley in *The Certain Hour*; and, of course, the immortal Jurgen and his delectable, evanescent loves in *Jurgen*.

Having said this much, it must be apparent that there is a "connecting theme" of these books. Again, in the author's own words, it is: "the lean and dusty axiom that human beings and human living are pretty much the same in most times and stations, and come by varying roads, as did Jurgen the pawnbroker and Manuel the high Count, to pretty much the same end." This idea *in extenso* may be found in the introduction to Cabell's ingenious conceit, *The Lineage of Lichfield.*

Coming now to Cabell's latest book, *The High Place*, we find him returning once more to his beloved mythical land of Poictesme, where the arch-philanderer, Jurgen, was born, and where tall, gray, squinting Manuel once ascended Vraidex.  The tale is of the time of the early 18th century (during the reign of le Grande Monarque) when your true gentleman, jauntily combining the qualities of knave and chevalier, possessed morals not quite so delicate as the Mechlin lace of his cravat.  And Florian, Duc de Puysange, hero of this romance and descendant in direct male line from Jurgen, is no exception.

The book tells of Florian's yearning to have for wife the beautiful Princess Melior, who had, according to Florian's later pronouncements, the intelligence of something between "a magpie and a turnip".  In order to gain possession of her for one year, Florian, by a mutually binding contract enlists the aid of brown Janicot, Satan's mundane henchman.  How Florian wins to Melior in the high place, weds her (thereby ultimately losing his cherished illusions regarding her character), and how his part of the bargain with Janicot is rendered void—all this, and more, is most entertainingly told with brilliant phrasing, diverting drollery, candid cynicism, and engaging frankness in the typical Cabellian manner.

To one reading between the lines, in this latest volume Cabell seems to say to the Comstockians: "If, forsooth, you consider *Jurgen* lewd, obscene and replete with double entendre (and you give the author complete credit therefor) here then is a book that may in all fairness be considered as possessing double entendre". For where in his books antedating *The High Place* Cabell's innuendoes have been neatly buried just underneath the surface, now the impish phrases peep puckishly forth from the verbal foliage as out-and-out double entendre. What a delectable raree-show *The High Place* promises for the acolytes of St. Anthony!

In this latest addition to the tales of Poictesme, Cabell seems to have come closer than ever to the style, the philosophy, the satire, and the cynicism of Anatole France,

for here he much more than touches the robe
of the French master. In the opinion of one
reader at least, *The High Place* will find a
lofty niche in the canon of the author's
productions, for it is by no means the dullest
star in that brilliant galaxy comprising the
Cabellian Milky Way.

Any commentator on Cabell's writings
would indeed be guilty of inexcusable neg-
ligence were he not to mention his poetry.
Perhaps it is news to many—even to some
of the cognoscenti—that this master of prose
has also written poetry. But he has—and
poetry of the first rank, forsooth. Dost not
believe? Then seek you out his lone volume
of published verse, *From the Hidden Way.*
You will have to make diligent search for it,
however, since it has been out of print for
nearly a decade (and now, by the way, is a
prized item eagerly sought for by collectors.)

In itself the book consists of seventy-five
so-called adaptations in verse, ostensibly
translated from medieval French and Italian
poets—but oh, what a merry hoax this is!
Yet apparently so genuine is Cabell's manner
of introducing his "translations", and so true

to the spirit of the periods they represent are the poems themselves, that few have guessed the existence of the deception. It is amusing to think that while writing and editing these verses for publication, Cabell had his tongue tilted in his cheek. And conceive you—the hoax fooled so erudite a gentleman as the book-reviewer of that bulwark of Brahminism, *The Boston Transcript!*

It may prove interesting to quote from Cabell's *Apologia Auctoris,* as he terms his preface to the book. Among other pungent things he says: "The grand power of poetry, in particular, is its interpretative faculty of so dealing with familiar things as to awaken a full and new sense of their strangeness." Rather an unusual definition—but none the less true in every respect.

To quote one lone excerpt from this too little known and meritorious volume is illadvised, since one should really read the contents in order to appreciate fully Cabell's ability as a poet. It adds at least a cubit and a half to his stature as a creative literary artist. However, lest we be considered parsimonious, here is one poignant bit of verse from the poem entitled "It Is Enough". This purports to have been written originally by Nicolas de Caen, which is, of course, but the name of one of Cabell's numerous poetic mimes appearing in the book.

The verse is as follows:

Of this I know not surely,—who am sure
That I shall always love you while I live,
And that, when I am dead, with naught to give
Of song or service, Love will yet endure,
And yet retain his last prerogative,
When I lie still, and sleep out centuries
With dreams of you and the exceeding love
I bore you, and am glad dreaming thereof,
And give God thanks for all, and so find peace,
        Yolande!

In passing, we may mention that Cabell has tried his hand at play-writing. *The Jewel Merchants* is a one-act play, having for its progenitor the short story entitled *Balthazar's Daughter*, contained in *The Certain Hour*. The fulcrum of this play, as noted by the author, is "the Renaissance conception of morality, which admitted of no recognition of criminality in crime, but only a perceptible risk." The historical personage around whom the play revolves is Alessandro de

Medici. Now in *The Jewel Merchants* Cabell has not written another *The Tinker's Wedding*, but he has at least produced an interesting, pleasing and artistic comedy (as he ironically terms it). It actually has an element of tragedy. It was first produced on the stage of the Little Theater of Richmond (Va.), Cabell's home city.

Another excursus of Cabell's into fields other than that of the novel or the short story is an essay called "A Note on Alcoves", appearing with eleven other essays by as many American authors, in the volume, *The Novel of Tomorrow*. This brief treatise contains some nice irony clothed with a felicity of phrase in the typical Cabellian manner, several caustic arrows discharged uneeringly at the Realistic School, and closes by voicing the opinions, first, that "the serious prose craftsman will write primarily to divert himself", and second, that the form and scope of the novel are "quite indeterminable".

Another essay, that our grandchildren will read and re-read with pleasure, is his Introduction to the Modern Library edition of that immortal story, *At the Sign of the Reine Pedauque* by Anatole France. It is eminently fitting that Cabell should thus fire a salvo in the great Frenchman's honor, since Cabell's skepticism regarding mundane affairs and his general ironic view-point are both quite reminiscent of M. France.

Maurice Baring says that Andrew Lang imagined the last man on earth will read the poems of Shelley in his cavern by the light of oil. With all due respect to the memories of Lang and Shelley, we imagine rather that, if the last man be an American, he will read (and chuckle over) his cherished copy of *Jurgen,* the masterpiece among Cabell's eighteen productions, and one of the greatest books ever produced in America.

Therefore, in closing let us give thanks to Jahveh that in these piping days of Babbittry we have here in the United States at least one creative literary artist, who, following in the tradition of the great ironic masters, Rabelais, Swift and Voltaire, has placed upon the altar of Literature jewels that will sparkle forever in the eyes of posterity.

# The Book of Life

BY

SAMUEL LOVEMAN

And sitting thus terribly enthroned, the heart of Jurgen was as lead within him, and he felt old and very tired. "For I do not know. Oh, nothing can help me, for I do not know what thing it is that I desire! And this book and this sceptre and this throne avail me nothing at all, and nothing can ever avail me: for I am Jurgen who seeks he knows not what."

*—Jurgen.*

# The
# Book of Life

JURGEN gives us in its semi-satiric, romantic amplitude the fecundity of the life-forces and of the procreative urge that is the very self and savour of life. Metaphorically it deals with the little half-pathetic fallacies that make illusion of existence, but in symbol it looms largely as a part of that literature veiled as yet to Western eyes, but entirely naked in its open candour to the Orient. Whether it be the darkened cone that Herodian tells us the young priest Elegabal danced before in a courtyard of a temple in Syria, or the lance that Jurgen breaks with Anaitis in his search for the adytum, the symbol remains the same.

Ever, the enormous shuttle creaks, and the diverse fabric woven is the same that Nature has enforced on her wayward and graceless puppets since there first appeared on the scene the perilous apparition of Time. *Jurgen* is clairvoyant with the subtlety and knowledge of these things. Mr. Cabell stands

in the wings with a half-tragic smile and a
not altogether dishumanizing attitude toward the delicate unreality of his world. But
whether his creatures love with vehemence or
sin with the audacity that their author could
only have given them in a fierce dissatisfaction
over the traditions that obstruct all freedom,
one must admit the verity of his art. That
verity is non-existent in much contemporary
writing.

*Jurgen* is equally the manuscript of the
Book of Youth and of Age. No other literature, certainly not that of the French
represented by M. Anatole France (with
whom Mr. Cabell has been most frequently
compared) can produce its like. You will
find quite obviously, as in M. Anatole France,
an irony at once delicate and sensual that
connotes very possibly the same flow from
the identical racial spring in the same lofty
region—but something has half-bewitched
and enfranchised the American writer into
a world at once alien and fantastic, yet still
eternally fanciful and terribly symbolic of its
own secret beauty. The Frenchman has the
sophistication of centuries and a weight of

lore and wisdom beside which Mr. Cabell may actually seem a neophyte, but of the sentiment that profoundly touches the hem of tragedy in *Jurgen,* you will discover in the former little, if anything at all.

And Mr. Cabell brings to the force and genius that make this book his masterpiece, an unparalleled elasticity of style, at times elliptical, at others veiled, and again, brilliant with its distinct empirical flame.

*Jurgen* is illusion, stripped chapter by chapter and page by page, until in "The Vision of Helen" with its blinding peroration to Beauty, or in the final chapter with Madame Dorothy on the dusked, moonlit terrace, a lyric materialism brings the book to a close. One finds pathos, comedy and the hugely exalted tragedy of sentiment. That is *Jurgen.* That is also, Life.

# Some Impressions
# of Cabell's Satire

BY

FRANK L. MINARIK

And everywhere, in every age, it seemed to him, men stumbled amiable and shatter-pated through a jungle of miracles, blind to its wonderfulness, and intent to gain a little money, food and sleep, a trinket or two, some rare snatched fleeting moments of rantipole laughter, and at the last a decent bed to die in. He, and he only, it seemed * * * * could see the jungle and all its awe-inspiring beauty, wherethrough men scurried like feeble-minded ants.

*—The Cream of the Jest.*

# Some Impressions
## of Cabell's Satire

"THERE is an Aristophanes in heaven", quotes Cabell, and in this trope is to be found the fundamental ethos which pervades all his works. However precisely or inaccurately this premise epitomizes the author's motif, nevertheless it may be safely stated that through such perspective of life he acquired his philosophy, or, if you will, vice versa. That such philosophy, which is at once a solvent of Man's foibles and a specific remedy for despair should find its most suitable vehicle in satire, is quite obvious.

Cabell's is an intimate understanding of the heavenly Aristophanes' formula and stagecraft of the human comedy. Even as this celestial jester, so does Cabell implant in the minds of his characters the delusive idea that makes each regard himself as the hub of the universe, and that each is his all-sufficient end. He arms them with the weapon of discriminating reason made impotent by impulse and emotion, and casts them, generally, in incompatible roles in which they maintain the propriety of their passions and caprices with arguments founded on passion and caprice.

Surely when filtered through an understanding such as this, satire strips itself of rancour and cynicism and takes on the garb of pity. Of such color and complexion is Cabell's satire. Tolerance and indulgence are woven into its texture and everywhere embroidered with a whimsy and fantasy that deprive it of seemingly direct accusation. This, say you, is a profitless motif. Yes, indeed. Artless art, that can make the theme double on itself and flaunt the formula and stage-craft in the very manner of the gods!

Trustingly you follow this master of satire into your Temple of Illusions and Prejudices at the very hour of twilight that begot them in your first remembrance. Reverently you pause before each shrine the while he interprets in hushed voice each symbol round the idol placed and you wonder at the profundity of this archeologist of your Olympus. How precisely he marks the genesis of these divinities, recounts their immortal deeds, interprets their very pose and tells with the warmth and ardor of a votary how rose the custom of mantling these idols so that only the contour of their facial features was exposed to mortal eyes.

The ceremony over, you walk arm in arm— for indeed, here was friendship born in common sympathies—to "the six tall windows upon the east side of the hall, those windows which are commingled blue and silver" but "now that the moon has risen" and "is clear of the tree tops" are an opulent glitter. " 'Twere a pity" says your new-found friend, "to shut out the fragrance of the garden that blooms beneath these windows. Should it not commingle with the incense of your sacrifice and do honor to your gods?" He opens the window and as the first gust of fragrant air pours into the temple you note the fitful flaring of the votive lamps, and in the brightness of their illumination you behold the disturbed mantles that clothe the idols, and in another fitful flare, their clay feet.

"Ah!" whispers your friend, as he quickly closes the window, "twere a pity to snuff out the votive lamp by so kindly an intention". And so you leave your friend, to wander homeward in the calm of the summer's night. The thought suddenly arrests you, "Why, 'twas a subterfuge when he did open the window to admit, forsooth, the garden's fragrance. 'Twas cunningly contrived that I should see what he seemingly did not disclose".

Yes, "there is an Aristophanes in heaven", and James Branch Cabell is his worthy interpreter and vicar!

*Bülg*
*the Forgotten*
BY
BEN RAY REDMAN

It is a law among us, for the protection of our youth, that "eating" must never be spoken of in any of our writing . . . . Ackermann, following Bülg's probably spurious text, disputes that this is the exact meaning of the noun.

—*Taboo*

# Bülg
## the Forgotten

IT IS curiously remarkable, in view of all the comment evoked from the public prints by the writings of James Branch Cabell, that there has appeared no adequate study of the sources from which this author has drawn material and inspiration. It is true that certain critics have accused Mr. Cabell of following the Stevensonian advice anent "the sedulous ape", and some have boldly prepared lists of the objects of his supposed imitation, but no one so far as I am aware has seriously considered the authors to whom more than to any others Mr. Cabell is admittedly indebted. What of his continuous borrowings from Codman, Lewistam, and Bülg? Mr. Cabell himself confesses his indebtedness to these three men, but no critic has troubled to appraise their involuntary loans.

One can only conclude that contemporary criticism is averse to scholarly employment; for Mr. Cabell has journeyed along literary bypaths that claim few followers, if any

beside him, in the present generation. It is
more than a hundred and twenty years since
Gottfried Johannes Bülg was acclaimed
throughout Europe as one of the most distinguished scholars of his day; Lewistam,
whose *Popular Tales of Poictesme* delighted
a select circle of our grandfathers, has passed
into oblivion; and Codman, the pillar of
erudition and the friend of Stewart and Reade,
enjoys only a splendid neglect from contemporary authors.  I hope that at some future
date, not too far distant, a competent critic
will exhume these forgotten worthies for the
sake of revealing the extent of their influence
upon Mr. Cabell.   But in awaiting this
desideratum, it seems well to present the
public  with  some  biographical notes  concerning one of the men upon whom Mr. Cabell
has leaned most heavily,—Gottfried Johannes
Bülg, the Max Muller of his day, now
utterly ignored.

What Max Muller did for India, Bülg was
once supposed to have done for Poictesme,
with the difference that Bülg commanded a
wider and more popular audience.  Why is

it then that his name, once a byword in
Europe, cannot be found in any of the three
most recent editions of the Encyclopaedia
Britannica, or in any biographical dictionary
of the last hundred years? Total eclipses of
this kind are rare in literature. Scarron was
studiously forgotten because he enjoyed the
unhappy honor of being the first husband of
her who became Madame de Maintenon and
virtual Queen of France. That is understand-
able. But what of Bülg? How is it that James
Branch Cabell should be the first author in
several generations to quote from his apparently erudite tomes?

The explanation of this phenomenon forms
one of the strangest chapters in the history
of literature. And, curiously enough, it is
an explanation of which Mr. Cabell himself
must be unaware, for otherwise he would not
have been imposed on by Bülg in the manner
hereinafter demonstrated. The facts to which
I refer are to be found only in various pamphlets which are now exceedingly rare because of the cheap and perishable paper upon
which they were printed. But if the pamphlets
themselves are lost, the purpose of their

authors has been accomplished. Bülg has been blotted out of history. He was exposed as a charlatan, and a charlatan, unless he be possessed of a most engaging personality, is soon unremembered by succeeding generations. For a time the name of Bülg was anathema; then it suffered the harsher fate of being totally forgotten. Not least among our debts to Mr. Cabell is his resurrection of this remarkable literary figure. That Mr. Cabell is ignorant concerning the true character of Bülg, however, is patent: Mr. Cabell accepts him at the estimate of a century and a quarter ago, unaware that posterity stripped from him his honors with a rough hand; and Mr. Cabell continues to quote from this revealed impostor with a faith that would be admirable were it inspired by a more worthy object. The few notes that I have collected here will serve to show the nature of the deception to which the author of *Jurgen* and *Taboo* and *The Lineage of Lichfield* has been subjected.

Gottfried Johannes Bülg was born in Strasburg in 1753 of prosperous, middle-class parents, and was educated at the University

of Leipsig, later attending lectures at Prague
and Tours. From his youth he was wild and
irresponsible, but possessed of a certain super-
ficial brilliancy which made him a prominent figure in student circles. It was in
Tours, at the age of twenty-five, that Bülg
met René Vincennes, an incident that was
pregnant with events. Vincennes was a
typical product of southern France, visionary,
enthusiastic, and capable of great affections.
The meretricious cleverness of Bülg attracted
this impressionable child of the south and
the two men, dissimilar as can be imagined,
swore undying friendship. It is obvious that
Bülg was the dominating figure in this asso-
ciation, quite overshadowing with his striking
personality the more profound but less showy
gifts of his companion.

Vincennes was above all a student. From
his early youth he had steeped himself in
the folk-lore and legends of Provence and
Poictesme, and at the time he met Bülg he
had virtually completed the manuscript of
a monumental and original work to be entitled *Poictesme en Chanson et Légende.*
He had devoted every faculty of an excep-

tionally endowed intelligence to this single effort, and with tireless pains and boundless enthusiasm had won his way toward its completion. He had explored a virgin field and the harvest had been rich indeed. Unmindful as he was of vulgar fame, he fully realized that the appearance of his three bulky volumes would mark an epoch in scholarship.

But the young Frenchman was cruelly destined not to reap his reward, for he was stricken with tuberculosis in its swiftest and most virulent form. On his death-bed he bequeathed the beloved work to his devoted friend, with minute instructions regarding its completion and subsequent publication. Bülg was the one person with whom he had shared his great secret, and never was a man more mistaken in his trust. After following Vincennes to the grave, Bülg set about one of the most contemptible thieveries in the history of literature.

Vincennes' work was a monument to diligent and scientific research, but it was not sufficiently sprightly to satisfy the imaginative German, whose faculties were stim-

ulated, we are informed, by frequent pota-
tions of laudanum; so the dishonest wretch
embroidered the volumes to his own liking,
filling them with fantastic tales and legends
which had never been known in any part of
Southern Europe, nor indeed elsewhere than
in his own drug-driven brain. With rare
ingenuity he altered the style in a manner
calculated to appeal to the general public as
well as to the scholarly audience for which
the work was originally intended. He then
translated the whole into German and published it under his own name in Strasburg,
in 1782. René Vincennes was safely buried.

The appearance of this notable work caused
a European sensation and Bülg, like Byron,
awoke one morning to find his fame firmly
established. There was one legend which
more than any other won for the work an
immediate popularity,—the tale of Jurgen.
The public in ordinary read it eagerly, and
pundits waxed hot in discussions concerning
the origins of Jurgen. Was he an actual hero
of a bygone age, or only a solar myth? Solar
myth or not, the name of Jurgen became famous and travelled to distant lands: while the

erudites searched for authorities, the public
was content to read. Curiously enough, the
Jurgen legend was one of the tales that Bülg
had distorted to such a degree that it bore
not the slightest resemblance to its original
form; even the name of the hero was a fanciful invention of his own. Mr. Cabell,
misled by Bülg, has perpetuated the error.

All, however, was not smooth sailing for
the perfidious author. There were puritanical
critics who found in the Jurgen legend, as
told by Bülg, an immoral symbolism, who
read into certain dubious passages dark and
curious meanings. Bülg chose to answer these
censors with an ingenuity which we might
admire had it not involved another literary
imposture. He published what purported
to be an authentic edition of *The Mulberry
Grove* by Saevius Nicanor, for the sake of
interpolating in the work a legend of his
own invention which was a satirical attack
upon his critics. Oddly enough it is this
interpolation which Mr. Cabell has brought
out under the title *Taboo*, undoubtedly in
complete ignorance of its significance in the
Bülg edition. Mr. Cabell has revived the text

from purely scholarly motives; Bülg forged
the original as a weapon against his puritanical
enemies.   He had stumbled upon the old
Dirghic legend, and seeing the opportunity
of twisting it into a defence of his Jurgen
epic, he ruthlessly mutilated the text to serve
his purpose.

The old Mansard edition of *The Mulberry
Grove,* to which Mr. Cabell refers in a biblio-
graphical note, had been completely lost,
and was known to Bülg's contemporaries only
through the comments of Garnier and some
others.   The current edition was that by
Tribebos, an honest enough work but marred
by carelessness.   Bülg took advantage of the
situation, denounced the Tribebos edition
as spurious, and announced that his own
edition was identical in all respects with the
Mansard version.   It was a fraud worthy of
the betrayer of Vincennes and during Bülg's
lifetime it completely deceived the public.   It
has apparently deceived Mr. Cabell also,
for he would never have chosen to resurrect
a villainously spurious document of this
character had he been informed regarding
the facts of the case.   Any one who is curious

enough to compare the Bülg and the Tribebos editions of *The Mulberry Grove* will immediately discover the interpolation, and will be able to appreciate how cleverly Bülg turned this weapon against the Grundys of his day. It is a pity that the Mansard edition of 1475 is lost, for reference to it would doubtless settle all discussions about the matter. But the main features of this daring forgery were exposed as long ago as 1825, when Vanderhoffen published his scholarly and vitriolic Introduction to the "restored" text of Saevius Nicanor.

It is impossible in this place to follow the career of Bülg subsequent to the publication of *The Mulberry Grove* in 1786, or to take notice of the various works which added lustre to his fame until death suddenly struck him down in the full prime of his dishonest success. Heart failure claimed Bülg unexpectedly in 1795, and the notes and manuscripts by Vincennes, which he had carefully preserved, and from which he culled his learning, revealed him to the world as the charlatan he was.

I am concerned with Bülg only in so far

as he has influenced and duped James Branch Cabell, and these few notes may suggest to some earnest student the possibility of further profitable research among Mr. Cabell's "authorities". It will assuredly repay his critics to do a little exploring, even if it leads them into strange and improbable ways. They must examine the voluminous works of Codman, Lewistam, Hahn-Kraftner, Garnier, Le Bret and Ackermann; they must spend dusty hours amid the verses of Riczi, Verville, Alessandro de Medici, Theodore de Passerat and many others; and, last of all, they must not neglect the 1620 edition of Burton's *Anatomy of Melancholy.*

*Some Rogueries*
*of James Branch Cabell*
BY
M. P. MOONEY

For the moral which I personally educe is that, in this world, wherein no fervor endures for a long while, and every clock-tick brings the infested tepid globe a little nearer to the moon's white nakedness and quiet, the wise will play while playing is permitted. The playthings will be words, because a man finds nowhere any lovelier toys.

*—The Lineage of Lichfield.*

# Some Rogueries
## of James Branch Cabell

THIS title implies nothing of which the penal statutes take cognizance. Nor is it intended thereby to charge the author with retailing to his readers anything that he has pilfered from others. On the contrary, his delightful deceits consist, to a large extent, of elaborate efforts to impose upon his readers as the work of others, the ingenious and curiously-wrought figments of his own brain.

The apparatus that he has constructed for this purpose is, in itself, a work of art; and many guileless readers must have spent valuable time in turning over the pages of encyclopedias, readers' guides and dictionaries of medieval romance and romance writers, in a fruitless effort to acquire further and authentic information about Jurgen, Dom Manuel, Horvendile and their associates. Only the most obtuse reader is unaware that these are, and are represented to be mythical personages, but even the acute and experienced reader may well be led to believe, under this author's fascinating guidance, that their singular adventures and heroic deeds, may have been the subject matter of at least oral tradition among the peasantry of Old France. This being assumed, there is nothing extraordinary in the reader believing that a host of commentators, glossators, and similarly harmless persons have spent a large part of their lives in the investigation and explication of these legends, and that the results of their labors are preserved in book form for the benefit of posterity. This innocent belief of the reader is, of course, confirmed by his knowledge of the fact that there is no legend, myth, saga, chanson, epic or ballade so obscure or unimportant as to lack its commentator. Whole libraries have been written around the legends of Charlemagne, Roland, Cuchulain, the Cid, Arthur, Ulysses, Siegfried and kindred real and imaginary personages, ancient and mediaeval, that have scarcely been heard of, much less read by that simple person "the general reader".

Here is surely fertile ground for a little literary roguishness, and Mr. Cabell is not the man to disappoint the expectations of

# A
# *Cabellian Comment*
## BY
## CHRISTOPHER MORLEY

Oh, certainly, Count Manuel's achievements were notable and such as were not known anywhere before, and men will talk of them for a long while. Yet, looking back,—now that this famed Count of Poictesme means less to me,—why I seem to see only the strivings of an ape reft of his tail, and grown rusty at climbing, who has reeled blunderingly from mystery to mystery, with pathetic makeshifts, not understanding anything, greedy in all desires, and always honeycombed with poltroonery.

—*Figures of Earth.*

his readers, or to weaken the plausibility of his narratives, when he can so easily produce the necessary supporting authorities.

Accordingly, there are paraded before the reader who is sufficiently diligent and thorough to read "prefaces" and "forewords", the fragmentary and sometimes controversial pronouncements of Dr. Codman, and Mr. Lewistam and Prote and Philip Borsdale anent these legends of Poictesme; while the "monumental" work of Angelo de Ruiz referred to in a very casual way is at least under suspicion.

Lord Dunsany, although writing in a land of romance where every river, hill and valley has its legend, and surrounded by a whole world of well-defined mythical characters, has seen fit to create a new race of legendary characters to serve as the dramatis personae in his plays and stories. While his work is undeniably well done, it suffers quite appreciably from the fact that his brood of new beings, with their strange and sometimes unpronounceable names, possess no connotation for the reader. The reader has never met them before; he has not been introduced to them; and while they perform acceptably the roles assigned them by the author, they pass across the stage leaving behind them no personality, no individuality.  Their action, their self-revelation, while they are doing their parts, are so meager and unsubstantial, that they and their names are forgotten as soon as they leave the scene.  In fact, while they are performing, they are little more than mere abstractions, requiring active mental effort on the part of the reader to endue them with any personality whatever.

Mr. Cabell, with fine artistic instinct, avoids these pitfalls.  Not for him is the tribe of robots that have no souls.  He prefers to deal with old and well-established legendary characters that the general reader has heard about. He knows that because of the concentrated curricula of our junior high schools and colleges, the names, at least, of some of these legendary personages will not be entirely unfamiliar to his readers; while he can count upon a certain vague knowledge of the legendary personalities on the part of many.  It is not good cultural form not to recognize at least the names of important legendary characters, and no one is so rude as to press for further details.

Where the author feels impelled to introduce new names or characters from the Scandanavian or the Celtic mythology, he seems to take special care that they shall bear a close orthographic resemblance to the accepted ones, so that the reader feels in a reminiscent way that he has heard of them before.    Therefore, perhaps unconsciously, Mr. Cabell bears fealty to a well-established principle of modern advertising that is practically applied in politics and business:  Lead the public to believe that it knows something favorable about your man or your article; that it has heard it before; repeat it often enough, then the public suffrage is assured.

In this way, Mr. Cabell gets a good start by using supposedly well-known and respectable characters; and the fantastic tricks that he makes them play as the story goes forward, do not in the  least detract from the interest or the merit of his book.  It is true that here and there a reader may be found who prides himself upon a more intimate acquaintance with some legendary hero or heroine, and who is shocked and grieved by Mr. Cabell's revelations concerning his favorite. One who might be disposed, in all charity, to say little or nothing about the Guenevere-Launcelot episodes, feels greatly pained and suspicious over the Thragnar incident, and inclines to lose his faith in legendary human nature as he peruses the evidence as to the activities of the Duke of Logreus prior to the coming of Arthur.

What fate awaits our author upon his arrival in the Elysian Fields, or Avalon, or Tir-na-nog, or other place to which such pagan authors go hereafter, must be matter for solemn speculation. Let us hope that his scandalized characters, like Niafer in *Figures of Earth* may "have tasted Lethe", and that thus his offenses will go unpunished because forgotten.

A peculiarly exasperating roguery of this author may be observed in *The Cream of the Jest*. We are here dealing with a case of apparently premeditated triple personality, the shifts from one to another being so frequent and unwarned that the reader suffers from vertigo. We remember that in Stev-

enson's *Dr. Jekyll and Mr. Hyde* the user of
the impure drug suddenly found himself
unable to control his change of personality,
with the serious consequences that followed
thereon. We suspect that Mr. Cabell's shifts
are purely voluntary, and intended to give
his reader all the sensations of incertitude
that he feels while striving to master Claude
Bragdon's expositions of the fourth dimension.
At times, the author seems to be speaking
in his own proper person. Suddenly, without
sounding a gong or blowing a horn, Felix
Kennaston takes up the burden and the author
disappears. Kennaston is a most unstable,
element, especially if he happen to glance
at the sigil of Scoteia; whereupon he sinks
into a trance, and the efficient agent becomes
our old friend Horvendile, who is surely a
fourth-dimensional character, judging by the
ease with which he slips in and out of three-
dimensional situations. These transforma-
tions occur so often that toward the end of
the book the reader is forced to believe that
the "cream of the jest" has no relation to the
sigil of Scoteia or its hypnotic power over
Kennaston, or its evocation of the phantoms

of Horvendile and "la Beale Ettarre", but consists entirely in Mr. Cabell's private joke upon his readers who, for nearly 300 pages are doing mental "loop-the-loops" until they discover the unromantic origin of the "sigil", and that Kennaston or somebody has been writing, and walking and talking in his sleep.

In *Penguin Island* Anatole France has given us one of the most amusing of modern books. Around the simple framework of the accidental baptism of a solemn colony of penguins, and their necessary transformation into human beings and Christians, he has built an ingenious and entertaining discussion of history, philosophy, religion, politics and social customs, which is carried on with that delightful urbanity and delicate satire so characteristic of that writer in nearly all his books. With a tolerant smile, he paints many of the foibles of humanity, and especially of those who for a brief time rise above the common level. Mr. Cabell finds himself unable to resist the temptation to do likewise, even at the moments when he seems most intent on romancing. If his books were undated, the student of political history would find little trouble in fixing their approximate date from these satirical touches. Note for instance, the chapter in *Figures of Earth,* where Count Manuel goes to a high secret place with the Princess Alianora and applies himself to the magic of the Apsarasas and brings multitudinous birds from all quarters of the sky, which begin immediately to give utterance to apothegms.  "So the eagle perched upon a rock and said tentatively, 'There is such a thing as being too proud to fight'; and again, 'The only enduring peace is a peace without victory'; and further, 'All persons that oppose me have pygmy minds'; and finally, 'If everybody does not do exactly as I order, the heart of the world will be broken'". We need no chorus to tell us who this "eagle" is.

Again the futility and inanity of modern conversation is satirized in at least one chapter of *The Cream of the Jest,* and no present reader who is more than twenty years old needs to be told what "great personage" uttered this daring piece of wisdom: "By George, there are many of our so-called captains of industry who, if the truth were told, and a shorter and uglier word were not unpermissible, are little better than malefactors of great wealth".

The author's chapter *Of Publishing* is a clever skit upon the supposed natural enemies of all authors, the publishers, and for all we "mute inglorious Miltons" may know, it possibly contains the essence of Mr. Cabell's private griefs against the publishing fraternity, remembered from the days when he was not the "best seller" he has since become.

A roguery that cannot long deceive the discerning reader is Mr. Cabell's propensity to scatter through his books the names of books written by his characters, with alluring titles of clearly Cabellian devising: *Men Who Loved Alison, The Audit at Storisende, As the Coming of Dawn, Ashtaroth's Lackey, In Scarlet Sidon, Through the Transom, The Tinctured Veil*, and such like. But though the reader be not deceived by this device he cannot fail to regret that such books have not been written by one who can "write perfectly of beautiful happenings", by the author of *The Certain Hour*.

There is no author that I can now recall, except Charles Lamb, that has so won my affection and interest by his felicities of style as has James Branch Cabell. Not that there is the least resemblance between these two authors. If any resemblance may be claimed to exist, it consists solely in the fact that Lamb, steeped in the drama and the sonorous prose of the Elizabethan age, wrote as an Elizabethan, yet with a distinctive style and turn of expression entirely his own.    Mr. Cabell seems similarly steeped in the romantic history of France and England at the period "when knighthood was in flower", and in the chronicles of those times, the very spirit and language of which he has absorbed and made his own. He has delved deeply into the capacities of the English language to express, "perfectly, beautiful thoughts and beautiful happenings", and his style, when he deals with these subjects is like that of no other modern writer of English. It has a beauty, a rhythm and a cadence that oftentimes is no longer prose, but poetry that sings in the reader's ear like sweet music.    And the sedulous reader of his books cannot fail to have noted that Mr. Cabell loves his own felicities, and that he quotes and re-quotes them at intervals and on suitable occasions in his books, so that the reader becomes conscious of them as of a recurrent musical phrase.

I do not speak of his sad but resigned pessimism on the subjects of love and marriage and allied topics as a "roguery". They may seem such to the young man and the young woman who have not yet drunk the full draught of life; but to those who have, his writings contain profounder truths than have so far been revealed to the entire tribe of psycho-analysts.

In conclusion:  I have spoken of Mr. Cabell's admirable and ornamented style when he writes on romantic subjects. This is his field and his peculiar department. *Beyond Life* is not a book by the Cabell that I know and enjoy.  But one bad apple in a bushel is not worth speaking of.

Needle-point tapestries, delicate laces, intricate embroideries in language;  these are the things that have given his admirers so much pleasure.   Let others weave the long rolls of coarse and unpatterned carpet, things that may be serviceable in a rude, everyday way, but possess no art.

# *A*
## *Cabellian Comment*

I CAN honestly claim to be a faithful appreciator of Mr. Cabell's curious talent: as long ago as 1916 I was writing in the public gazettes in his honor. *Beyond Life* is perhaps my favorite among his books (of those I've read) I admit that I have not read *Jurgen*, as the hullabaloo about it wearied me. When I was offered Ten Dollars for my copy of the first edition, I sold it, with a feeling of having done well.

The special kind of farcical fantasy that Mr. Cabell has made his province seems to me eminently faithful to the essence of medieval humor, which was pungently grotesque. His ramblings in the land of Poictesme are a crazy-quilt of medieval colors: and not intended to be literal and point-device in the hemstitching. They are full of an agreeable skittishness, much of which is far too subtle for the casual flitter-mice among readers. In *Figures of Earth* (a delicious book) there is much buried wit over which Cabell has scratched a little gold-dust; it is by no means evident. There is finely-wrought irony and purgatory mirth which will both escape most of his readers. Mr. Cabell, it is plain, stands among the scoffers; but he scoffs not merely as a cynic; he grins, but not, as Scripture says, like a dog. He has command of tenderness, and of occasional haunting refrains of loveliness. He enters the forest-aisles of medieval romance in the spirit of Our Lady's tumbler. Perhaps it is as a poet that I esteem him most of all; there is no more glittering pen now available for a maliciously tender and passionate love sonnet.

# A Note on the
# Poetry of James Branch Cabell

BY

EDWIN MEADE ROBINSON

The grand power of poetry, in particular. is its interpretative faculty of so dealing with familiar things as to awaken a full and new sense of their strangeness.

*—From the Hidden Way.*

# A Note on the Poetry
## of James Branch Cabell

I DO not know why the verse critics and poetasters have approached Cabell so gingerly. People who know little about the matter seem inclined to deny him the title of poet—which only shows that they cannot properly savor his prose. Louis Untermeyer did not discover *From the Hidden Way* until 1920, though the book had been published in 1916, and so left Cabell out of the first edition of *Modern American Poetry*, which was published in 1919. Then he sought to remedy his omission by an enthusiastic, if somewhat careless, article in *The Literary Review*, and here he lays much stress—too much—upon the Cabell "hoax".

Now let us get the hoax out of the way at the start. *From the Hidden Way* purports to be a collection of adaptations from the Provencal troubadours. The name of the supposed author of each poem is given, and usually the first line or so in the original Langue d'oc, Provencal, Italian, old French or Latin. The

names of none of these poets are familiar
to the reader. A search among the libraries
reveals them not at all. Cabell has hoaxed
us, as did MacPherson and Chatterton.

It is not, however, a matter for indignation
(except on the part of certain reviewers who
accepted these "translations" in good faith
and hinted at their own perfect familiarity
with the originals). The deception is an
intimate and necessary feature of the entire
Cabell Romance. When you shall have discovered the complete records of the realm
of Poictesme you will find the biographies of
these poets religiously preserved by the ancestors and descendants of Duke Jurgen.
They belong to mythology. They are songs
indigenous to that delectable region and contemporary with that golden age. To call them a
hoax is equivalent to denying the historicity
of *The High Place* and casting doubt on
the archives of Duke Logreus and Mother
Sereda. Annoyed critics should read *Beyond
Life* more critically.

To me it seems quite natural that having
invented an era and a kingdom Cabell should
have furnished it with a more or less complete

lyric literature. And having made himself a spiritual home in a world of his own creation, how otherwise could he write his poetry? These ballads are irregular in form. These *planhs* and *sirventes* are inventions. I thought at first to criticise the technique of certain fixed forms, but by his very method and preparation the poet has put such details beyond my criticism. Is the *rime parfait* used freely? Thus was it in the old days. Are rhyme words repeated? They wrought not otherwise in Poictesme. Are these rondels in other ways according to the troubadours? The poets were a lawless lot, of old time. We are helpless.

So the criticism must get right down to the meat of the matter—are these songs real poetry? Is their technique effective, though petty rules be broken? Are they musical, are they beautiful, are they something more than imitations of sentiment, parodies of the medieval style, cleverly built echoes of a by-gone age?

And the answer must be that they are real poems. They are not among my favorites, except in rare moods; few of them are unforgetable; there is a sameness about them;

they repeat the ideas and perplexities and disillusionments of the novels; but they are instinct with Romance; they are perfumed; they sing, they weep, they are a part of the author's own nature; they never leave the realm of pure poetry.

As Cabell made out a case for Romance in *Beyond Life*, so he makes out a case for the medieval poetry in his *Apologia Auctoris* which prefaces *From the Hidden Way*; and he does it quite briefly, epigrammatically and thoroughly. If his reasoning sounds like Chesterton's (and it does, very remarkably), it is none the less sincere for that, and none the less effective. Similarly, if some of his verse sounds like Rossetti and Morris and Swinburne, it is because those poets, too, immersed themselves in the medieval singers— in Villon and Charles d'Orleans and the others. They have sucked the same milk and learned the same accent. I call your attention to "Marcus Aurelius," on page 33 of *From the Hidden Way*; were it unsigned you would attribute it to Swinburne; and "False Dawn in Troy" might be Morris.

But I multiply words to no effect. The sum of the whole matter is this—that the poetry of Cabell is something you may like or dislike or even ignore, for it belongs to a restricted audience. You must medievalize yourself to like a large portion of it. It can never be popular; it will never be vastly important. But do not be deceived into thinking that it is second-rate stuff on the one hand, or obscure and esoteric stuff on the other hand; or that it is imitation. It belongs to a mood, and in that same mood its author has written the best of his books. Only when the mood deserts him does he seem not quite himself.

As a foot-note in conclusion, let me return to Untermeyer's *Literary Review* article. He says: "He has even gone to the extent of inserting a technically perfect sonnet in a conversation. The curious may find this tour de force disguised as prose on the 97th page of *Jurgen*." Well, I have been through page 97 with a magnifying glass and a fine-toothed comb, and I find no sonnet. There is a poem there disguised as prose, but only by an impossible elasticity of definition can it be called a sonnet at all. It is a *sirvente*, as Jurgen announces on page 95, and a *sirvente* (or at least this one) has 14 lines all ending with the same word. The 14 lines are iambic pentameter, but if this is all that is necessary to make a "technically perfect" sonnet, the rules have all been suspended. I think that Untermeyer can not have had the book by him when he made this statement.

# James Branch Cabell
# and William Jennings Bryan
BY

HOWARD WOLF

"Life is short", the wise men tell us,
Even those dusty, musty fellows
That have done with life—and pass
Where the wraith of Aristotle
Hankers, vainly, for a bottle,
Youth and some frank Grecian lass.

—*The Line of Love.*

## James Branch Cabell
## and William Jennings Bryan

HE AIM of the following essay is to illustrate and to prove the proposition that all human beings are curiously alike. Despite the most earnest striving, any attempt at becoming somehow different from any other mortal never amounts to more than a gesture, magnificent it may be, but pitiful in its futility. In support of my contention I offer for your inspection two gentlemen as utterly unlike each other as it is possible for any two of us to be. Both are eminent Americans, but there the resemblance would seem to end. One is widely renowned as a temperance orator and religious leader, a distinguished kisser of babies who has successfully rivalled trained seals and Swiss bell-ringers on many high-class Chautauqua programs. The other is a retiring gentleman known only to a small portion of the populace of this country, and by them hailed variously as poet, pander, iconoclast and menace to youthful purity. Superficially considered, these two citizens would seem to possess absolutely nothing in common. But upon closer examination, how strangely they resemble each other after all!

For instance—despite opinions to the contrary Mr. Cabell and Mr. Bryan, in reality, are both conspicuous moralists. William Jennings is, of course, widely known as an advocate of virtue. Cabell has been much maligned. It pains me to hear of his being hailed as a poisonous python, coiling around the pure youth of the nation and strangling its embattled innocence. I am amazed that no one has risen to protest against the persistently circulated calumny and scandal which has undermined the reputation of as noble a man as ever brandished his staff in defence of morality. It has been said that Stephen Crane's *Red Badge of Courage* bristles with as many grammatical errors as with bayonets. Of a verity, *Jurgen* bristles with as many moral lessons as with lances. I advocate placing it in every schoolroom in the land. In comparison with the polite Jurgen, the highly touted little Rollo was a blundering oaf. For a lesson in courtesy what would appeal to the young reader more than the tale of how our Duke of Logreus chivalrously came to the aid of Dame Yolande? How could the youngster be more forcefully impressed with the importance of his school work and the necessity for study than by hearing how Jurgen's knowledge of mathematics assisted him in his dealings with the Queen of Philistia? What better training for his imagination than mention of the moving ceremony known as the Breaking of the Veil? I am confident that the study of this volume would immeasurably elevate the literary quality of those quaint legends which schoolboys chalk upon convenient walls on their way home from classes. "Teacher is an Anaitis!" "Our Principal was once as we are!" Such announcements would replace those now in use, which betray an unusual lack of inventiveness.

But to proceed with the comparison, Bryan and Cabell are both masters of platitude. Bryan in all his speeches. Cabell in his books, notably *Jurgen*. This I adduce as one proof of the greatness of the scrivener of Dumbarton Grange. There are more platitudes in the writings of Shakespeare than are to be found in the works of any other author. That, in itself, is a platitude. Shakespeare was the first to say a number of things which have since become platitudes, but his plays abound with speeches which were truisms when he first made use of them. *Jurgen*, similarly, advances many ancient sentiments, but always tricked out in such admirable phrasing that they glitter like new. Our author is continually playing Lady Bountiful to some poor little ragamuffin of a platitude picked up in the slums of literature. After he has, lovingly, washed the grimy face, slicked down the disordered hair and appareled the waif in a brand-new suit of clothes, neat but not gaudy, the child is almost unrecognizable. As a result of the great transformation scene we have a very Lord Fauntleroy of a phrase before which common, grubby little adjectives, verbs and nouns tip their caps in awed respect. Cabell, I consider to be the first author since Shakespeare capable of wording his platitudes with such consummate magic and beauty that they startle us with their freshness.

Carrying my original analogy still further I believe that in the matter of literary opinions Mr. Cabell and Mr. Bryan would most heartily concur. Somewhere in *The Judging of Jurgen* Cabell makes a statement to the effect that Edgar, Walt and Mark are the only great literary artists whom this country has produced. By this somewhat cryptic utterance he undoubtedly intends to refer to Edgar A. Guest, Walt Mason and Edwin Markham. If this estimate fails to meet with Mr. Bryan's vociferous approval I shall be greatly amazed.

And now for my most telling point which I have reserved to conclude this little study. Both of the gentlemen are incurable Romanticists, gallant champions of picturesque yesterdays, in perpetual revolt against the dull gray materialism of the present—Cabell bearding the Lions' Club, Bryan defying Darwin. Are these not astoundingly similar spectacles? Cries Herr Bryan in effect: "Away with this Darwin theory! I refuse to believe that our original mother was a shaggy, repulsive ape. This modern idea is revolting to me. I stand for the old-fashioned

seductive Eve!   The Eve of romance and
tradition strutting her stuff in the Garden.
A beautiful woman, by God, reclining in an
inviting posture, with only a fig-leaf
concealing her colophon!"   Senor Cabell,
likewise, repudiates all things that smack of
modernity.   Determinedly, he turns his back
on all present-day things, and engages in
queer traffic with alluring ghosts of faintly
remembered far-off times.   In *Beyond Life*
he advances the theory that an author should
never deal with a contemporary setting.   In
the best of his own works he adheres to this
dictum.   The novels of present-day Southern
life are, without question, his weakest per-
formances.   *Chivalry*,   *Domnei*,   and   the
best of the stories in *The Line of Love* and *The
Certain Hour* deal with historical days and
are woven of high imaginings of the beauty
of times past.   *Jurgen* and *Figures of Earth*
breathe of the mythology which is of all time,
but despite ironical references to modern
events and personages the illusion of anti-
quity is always maintained.   *The Cream of
the Jest* is ostensibly a story of modern life
but the high spots of the book are the vig-

nettes of vanished periods.   Always, when
most himself, this Cabell is an old lover of
the glamour and pageantry of by-gone days,
pondering over his glittering dreams in the
manner of the faded ladies in Victorian
novels, who hourlong shuffle their packets
of yellowed letters, broodingly oblivious
of aught else in their contemplation of some
once hectic moment. Imaginative Bryan,
dallying with dead Eve. Cabell dreaming
of assorted Phyllisses, Dorothys and
Gueneveres. Are they not, at least, brothers
under the skin?

# The Style of Cabell

BY

## H. L. MENCKEN

"Your style," the Duke regretfully observed, "is somewhat more original than your subject."
—*Gallantry*

# The Style of
# Cabell

WHAT one finds, above all, in the books of James Branch Cabell is the thing vaguely called style—the painter's alert feeling for form and color, the musician's sensitiveness to rhythm. The thing said, though often it is excellent, is of secondary consideration; of chief importance is the way of saying it. And that right way of saying it goes further than a mere choice of felicitous adjectives, arresting epithets, *mots justes*; it extends to the sentence as a whole, to the chapter as a whole, to the book as a whole; there is an adept search for the right measure, the right cadence, the right procession of colors. Reading Cabell, one always gets a sense of harmonious flow. The inner ear responds to a movement that is subtly correct and satisfying. There is no hesitation and there is no cacophony.

What lies under that music—and often the measures themselves are so charming that one scarcely looks beneath them—is the quality of irony, as rare in American

writing as distinguished style—the somewhat
disdainful detachment of a man who is beyond taking his fable too seriously, but not
beyond sensing every atom of its comedy.
Cabell is too wise a bird to believe that fairy
tales are important.  He knows quite well
that a world rid of story-tellers might yet
remain a world full of dreams.  But if he
does exalt his office too much, he at least
respects its duties.  While he serves, he will
serve diligently.  So what cannot be made
portentous, he tries at least to make amusing
and lovely, and almost always he succeeds.
His manner is that of a highly accomplished
and resourceful artist; his philosophy is that
of a highly civilized man.  The Comstocks,
it seems to me, judge him very accurately.
He is their relentless and formidable enemy,
even when he seems to be cooing like a dove;
in every line he writes there is contumacy
to their brummagem revelation.

The appearance of such a man in the
America of the Fundamentalists, the Ku
Klux Klan and the Wilson idealism is a
phenomenon of a scandalous and extremely

gratifying variety. It is more than an accident; it is a sort of occult retribution or act of God. The Republic, having decided solemnly to put down all artists, finds itself entertaining strangely an artist of the first calibre. Intelligence being formally adjourned, it pops up suddenly in, of all places, the late Confederacy! There is irony here to delight Cabell himself. He has been his own hero, of course, since his first book. But when he grows old at last, and sits down to tell his story in the first person, it will be richer in humor, I believe, and more compact with a lush and sardonic immorality, than the stories of a dozen Jurgens.

# A Letter
# concerning Jurgen

BY

BURTON RASCOE

"*  *  *  *  all progress, I would have you note, is directed by wise persons who discreetly observe the great law of living—"

"And what is that law, monsieur, my father?'"

"Thou shalt not offend", the Duke replied, "against the notions of thy neighbor. Now to the honoring of this law the wise person will bring more of earnestness than he will. bring to the weighing of discrepancies between facts and well-thought-of ideas about these facts. So, at most, he will laugh, he will perhaps cast an oblique jest with studied carelessness: and he will then pass on, upon the one way that is safe—without ever really considering the gaucherie of regarding life too seriously. And his less daring fellows will follow him by and by, upon the road which they were going to take in any event. That is progress."

—*The High Place.*

# A Letter
# concerning Jurgen

## New York Tribune
### New York

January 12, 1924

My dear Mr. Bregenzer:-

Regarding a contribution for the symposium, I am afraid I am too late—I've been frightfully busy—but!

I had rather have *Jurgen* by James Branch Cabell dedicated to me than be the dedicatee of any book published during the past ten years, in English or in any other language. And, since that honor came to me quite unexpectedly, I feel definitely certain that my name, if only in so far as it figures on the dedicatory page of one book, will not be as one writ in water for some centuries to come.

Sincerely,

(Signed) BURTON RASCOE.

# "*From the Hidden Way*"

BY

CARR LIGGETT

"No," she answered slowly, "there is a thing called love * * * * "To a man," she went on, dully, "it means to take some woman—the nearest woman who isn't actually deformed—and to declaim pretty speeches to her and to make her love him. And after a while—" Kathleen shrugged. "Why, after a while", said she, "he grows tired and looks for some other woman".

—*The Eagle's Shadow.*

## "From the Hidden Way"

**Y**OU who have sung to a silver lyre
  Ballads of ladies strangely sweet
  Leave me sorrowing at your feet
Touched by too lovely lyric fire.
I have wept for each dead desire,
  Long laid under the cypress bough;
  Ah, could I woo them, even now
I might be Lord Love's singing squire.

Dorothy the forever young;
  Adelais the forever fair;
  Sylvia wise and debonair
Past all words from my halting tongue;
Chloris the daintiest among
  All Time's sweethearts and ah, too fond;
  Felise of dreams and rare Yolande—
Fadeless beauty divinely sung.

You who have dwelt in Arcady,
  You who have breathed its fragrant night,
  Sought these bringers of mad delight,
Blithely bowed to their tyranny,

Yours is an ageless minstrelsy:
  Mocked are the lovers who pipe a day;
  Jurgen sings as but Jurgen may
Out of the moonlight, deathlessly.


EXPLICIT

www.ingramcontent.com/pod-product-compliance
Lightning Source LLC
LaVergne TN
LVHW011243080426
835509LV00005B/618

*9 7 8 1 4 3 4 4 9 4 8 5 6 *